W9-BVT-266

Jaclynn Schaap Weber

No Regrets

Copyright © 2004
CHRISTIAN WOMANHOOD
8400 Burr Street
Crown Point, Indiana 46307
(219) 365-3202

ISBN 0-9745195-4-5

All Scriptures used in this book are
from the King James Bible.

CREDITS
PROJECT MANAGER: Dan Wolfe
COVER DESIGN & PAGE LAYOUT: Linda Stubblefield
PROOFREADING: Rena Fish
PHOTOGRAPHY: Larry Titak, Schererville, Indiana
TYPIST: Yashinca Pontillas

PHOTOS:
Cover: Todd and Jaclynn on their wedding day
Title page: Dr. and Mrs. Jack Schaap
with Todd and Jaclynn Weber

Table of Contents

Preface
by Dr. Jack Schaap

If there is a more satisfying pleasure for a parent or a more gratifying honor for a father than the one I received on the wedding day of Todd Weber and Jaclynn Schaap, I can't imagine what it could be.

I was honored to perform their wedding as both their pastor and as Jaclynn's father. As I waited with my daughter for the signal to escort her down the aisle where I would give her away, she said, "Dad, when you pronounce Todd and me as husband and wife and we kiss, it will be our very first kiss ever."

I looked at her in her beautiful wedding gown and realized that I was looking at a rare treasure.

Here was a virgin young lady who was deservingly wearing that white dress, a symbol of her purity. She had kept her promise to her mother and to me when we had given her a purity ring many years earlier, and now she was presenting herself as a chaste virgin to her groom.

He too had protected his life and yielded his body to be pure to his wedding day. They were gifts both earned and given by and for each other.

Mrs. Schaap and I have often said to each other that Jaclynn was a rare gift from God to us. She nearly died at birth. The umbilical cord had wrapped around her neck twice and had starved her brain of oxygen. Shortly afterward, the delivery doctor told me that our little newborn girl had probably suffered brain damage and would be quite handicapped.

A few days later, I was allowed to hold her for the first time. As I took her into my arms, I whispered into her tiny ear, "Jaclynn, this is Daddy. Everything's all right now; Daddy's here." From that moment, our hearts were forever knit.

Jaclynn was not handicapped. In fact, she was

a fabulous student, graduating number three in her high school class. Jaclynn has possessed from early years a profound zeal for doing right, and she developed a very close walk with God from a child.

We knew it would take a rare young man to provide the leadership and quiet strength for Jaclynn to follow. God gave her such a man in Todd Weber. He too had learned to walk with God and to discipline his life in purity and holiness. What a gift he has been for Jaclynn; what a fine son-in-law he is to Mrs. Schaap and me. How very pleased we are in both of them.

If every father could be made to feel as Jaclynn has made me feel, if every father and mother could know the joys that Jaclynn has brought us, and if every parent could be as pleased with their daughters as we are with Jaclynn, then every parent would be the happiest of people.

I commend to you this book and its author, both of which are worthy of your study.

"It's a Wonderful Life!"

"Blessed is the man that walketh not in the counsel of the ungodly, nor standeth in the way of sinners, nor sitteth in the seat of the scornful. But his delight is in the law of the LORD; and in his law doth he meditate day and night. And he shall be like a tree planted by the rivers of water, that bringeth forth his fruit in his season; his leaf also shall not wither; and whatsoever he doeth shall prosper."

(Psalm 1:1-3)

Chapter One

It's a Wonderful Life!

The story of my life is nothing really exciting; in fact, it is very normal. I was born into a godly, Christian family with parents who loved me and cared for me, and who obviously loved each other very much. I started going to church when I was two weeks old and rarely ever missed a service.

I was taught about Jesus, standards, and right and wrong from the time I was born, and it has been drilled into my head consistently each year. My mom led me to the Lord when I was four years old, and I was baptized a few weeks later. Since he was a preacher, my dad baptized me; I kicked and screamed when I realized that he was about to put my head under water! However, the water was very warm; and after it was over, I wanted to do it again! I grew up in the Christian school that my grandfather started, went to the church that he pastored, and had a preacher and a teacher for parents.

I went on to graduate from Hammond Baptist High School and attended the college that my grandfather had also started. The thought of going anywhere else was out of the question. Aside from what everyone else would have thought of "Dr. Jack Hyles' granddaughter" going somewhere else, I would never have been able to handle the disappointment of my grandparents and parents if I had gone to another school.

While in college, I met a tall, dark, handsome man whom I married three years later; and of course, he wanted to be a preacher. We both graduated from Hyles-Anderson College, and we are now teachers, too.

This is the story of my life up through today. I have no thrilling stories of years wasted out partying and sowing my wild oats, no near-death experiences when I asked God to give me just one more chance to give my heart to Him, no emotional roller coaster of getting into trouble with the wrong guy and having to pay for it, and really nothing out of the ordinary for a Christian teenager. When I was a teenager, often I would hear testimonies of people who lived wild, "exciting" lives for years; then one day finally decided to give it all up for the Lord. Sometimes I thought to myself, "Their life sounds exciting, and they have such a great story to tell everyone," and I would wonder what it would be like to do some of those daring things.

In February 2004, a man named Keith Cowling gave his testimony in church during the morning service, and his testimony was very similar to mine. He grew up in a Christian home, went to a Christian school, married a Christian girl, and works at the college that my grandfather started and where his parents also work. He has no wild stories about years wasted with alcohol, drugs, or anything else, and he has led a pretty normal life, too. His story made me think about my testimony and where I am in life, and I realized again what a great story and an incredible heritage I have.

The truth is, I would rather have my story than the story of the person who has gone into sin and has experienced the wildest things this world has to offer. During a spring program at First Baptist Church, we had people give testimonies every Sunday morning and Sunday night for quite a few weeks, and many of their stories were about going into deep sin and finally giving in to God. Yes, they are happy now, but they all say the same thing: "I wish I would have given my life to God a long time ago and never wasted all of those years." Each one of them feels that God can use him, but never like He could have used him had he listened the first time to God's voice. They all have regrets and wish they could do some things over again.

After hearing Brother Cowling's testimony, I took a look at my story and realized how exciting it really is and how happy doing right has made me. No, I will never travel the world for people to hear of my thrilling adventures and how God spared my life to serve Him, and it is probably not the most exciting story you will ever hear. To me though, it is as thrilling as the wildest roller coaster you could ever ride, more exciting than going to Hawaii or seeing Niagara Falls, or going skydiving. It is more beautiful than watching the sun rise over the Grand Canyon or lying underneath a starry night sky in the Rocky Mountains. It is exciting because I know God created me with a special purpose, and He placed me here for a reason, and by His grace, I have been spared from Satan's ruining of my life. I am the happiest girl alive today, and I think my story is the most exciting one I have ever heard.

No One Understands Me!

*"How precious also are thy thoughts unto me,
O God! how great is the sum of them! If I
should count them, they are more in number
than the sand: when I awake,
I am still with thee."*
(Psalm 139:17, 18)

Chapter Two

No One Understands Me!

Whoever said being a teenager is easy must have skipped that step! It's true that junior high school and high school are fun, but they can be some of the hardest years that a person faces.

Many of you teenagers have had parents divorce or even die. Some of you have brothers or sisters who have a disease and have a lot of problems. Some of you have problems at home with parents fighting all of the time. Some of you have siblings who have broken your parents' hearts. Some of you have probably been abused, and as a result, you feel like no one understands you. Most

of you have or have had problems with friends or boyfriends, or you have experienced peer pressure at school. If you are in a public school, you deal with a lot more than peer pressure.

However, no matter what you face, every teenager has one thing in common: you feel like NO ONE understands what you have been through or no one cares. Many of you rebel or get bitter at God or your parents because of things that happen to you, and you miss out on so many things that are waiting in the future.

I once heard someone say, "Every teenager goes through a rebellious stage at some point in his life." That statement may or may not be true. I do agree that every teenager at some point has hard times and may have a reason to rebel, but I also think that there is a way to get through the hard times without getting bitter or ruining your life.

My sophomore year of high school was definitely my hardest year. What I remember most about that year was that I cried a lot, and I did not like school. I know there were some good points, but for many reasons it was a rough year. I remember feeling very lonely at times, and like many of you, I felt like no one understood me. No one was going through exactly what I was going through, and no one is going through exactly what you are going through—no one except for God.

No one understands you completely except for the One Who created you, saved you, and is with you in every class, at every party, during every day and every night. He is the one Person Who never leaves you, Who knows every thought and dream you have, and Who knows the real you who is hidden deep down inside your heart. And He is the only One Who can help you make it through EVERY problem that you have.

Yet to many of us, He is as much of a stranger as the man we pass walking down the street. He is so close to us, but we are so far from Him. Why are we so blind that we never stop to think that Jesus loves us and wants us to make it? He was good enough for us when we were in kindergarten, but now that we are "mature teens" who think we have everything under control, we really don't have any use for Him anymore.

During my sophomore year, when I thought I would never make it and was all alone in the world, I had no one to turn to but God. That is when I began to find out how real He is and how much He cares for me. I would cry and cry, and through my tears I would open my Bible and read the book of Psalms over and over. I would under-line every verse that talked about how special I was to God and how much He loved me. I would talk to Him through tears and beg Him to help me through that day.

Psalm 139 became my favorite chapter because it describes God's love to me. *"How precious also are thy thoughts unto me, O God! how great is the sum of them! If I should count them, they are more in number than the sand: when I awake, I am still with thee."* (Psalm 139:17, 18) These verses mean that God thinks about me more times than the number of grains of sand on the shore. Have you ever been to the ocean and tried to count the grains of sand? (I'm sure that's what you love to do in your spare time!) Well, I'll just say there are a lot more than you could ever count, and that number represents a lot of thoughts that God thinks about you and me!

If God loves you that much, then I am sure He can help you with whatever problem you are facing. Having a relationship with God is not just for old people—it's for you, and I challenge you to get to know Him, and you won't have to go through a "rebellious" stage.

My Mother, My Friend?

"Honour thy father and thy mother: that thy days may be long upon the land which the LORD thy God giveth thee."
(Exodus 20:12)

Chapter Three

My Mother, My Friend?

The following are some common phrases I have heard teenage girls say about their mothers:

- "My mom just doesn't understand me."
- "My mom and I can't shop together; she has absolutely no taste in clothes."
- "My mom never listens to me; she's always yelling at me."
- "I hate my mom."

On the other hand, these are some phrases I have heard other teenage girls say about their mothers:

- "My mother is my best friend."
- "My mom and I do everything together."
- "My mom is my role model."

- "I can tell my mom anything; she listens to me."

Now obviously what some girls said was drastically different from what others said, yet I believe these teenagers are very much alike. Most of them have similar backgrounds; most have grown up in Christian homes, and all of them have parents who love them and want the best for them. If they are so much alike in so many ways, why then do they feel so differently about their mothers? I know that everyone is different and has unique circumstances, but I think there are some ways teen girls can make their moms their best friends and thereby avoid years of fighting and stress.

When I was a little girl, my mom was just that—my mom. She told me when to eat, when to sleep, when to take a bath, and even when to go to the bathroom! She was my teacher, and she was in complete control of my life.

Then slowly, without hardly even noticing, I began to do those things on my own, and Mom told me less and less what to do and when to do it. I became more and more independent, and I began to see her more as my friend than my mom.

By the time I started high school, I felt very much like my mom was my best friend. We did lots of things together, and many times I felt like we were on the same level in our relationship. This stage is where problems can arise. I wanted her to be my friend, but I no longer wanted her to tell me what to do. I was 16 and already had my driver's license, which in my mind made me practically an adult. I didn't like it when Mom told me what to do. However, Mom didn't seem to think I was ready to be on my own, and she kept right on telling me what to do.

I believe this can be the most stressful time for a mother and a daughter; yet if you, as a teenage girl, will learn to accept the fact that your mom, who sometimes seems like your closest friend, is still your mom, then I think the two of you could have a great relationship. I had to learn that I was young and dumb, and that she had been through what I was going through—dating, the breakups, the friend problems, and every emotional change I was experiencing. I learned that if I would talk to her and ask her advice, she really could help me.

Now I know that some of you do not have the ideal home situation, and that fact definitely complicates things. Yet, you too can have a great relationship with your mom or stepmom. When one of my friends was having problems with her stepmom, my friend just decided to make her stepmom feel like she loved her as her own mother (which was difficult). As a result, she realized her stepmom really did love her and wanted so much to be a part of her life.

Now that I am married, my mom is very much my friend, but I know that she will always be my mom. I am still very young, so I know that when she tells me what to do, I need it, whether or not I think I do. You really should get to know your mom because she's the best friend you have!

She Is So "Holy"

"For I am the LORD your God:
ye shall therefore sanctify yourselves,
and ye shall be holy; for I am holy...."
(Leviticus 11:44)

Chapter Four

She Is So "Holy"

When I was in high school, it was not popular to be a part of the really "bad" crowd, yet no one wanted to be the "holy" crowd either. I always knew I was going to attend Hyles-Anderson College (as if I had a choice!), marry a preacher, and serve God full time with my life, but in high school that goal seemed so far away. I did not feel the "burden" to save America and often felt like God was somewhere around, but not that close to me. I always hung around the "good" crowd, but I got along with the so-called "bad" crowd, too.

By the time I was a senior in high school though, I was thinking more seriously about my future and where I was headed in life. At school

camp that year on Wednesday night, a group of us girls went down by the lake and prayed a long time for our class. We prayed that some big decisions would be made and that some lives would be changed. I remember feeling that night that God was very close to us and to me, and I felt very burdened for our class and our school.

Well, Thursday night, the last night of camp, came and went, and though a lot of good decisions were made, many were not, and we felt like our prayers were pointless. Little did we know at the time how much God heard our prayers and would answer them in the future. Many of those classmates for whom we prayed are now happily married and in full-time Christian service, and almost all of them are very involved in church.

I realized something that night as we prayed by the lake—something that would make a remarkable difference in my life. I realized that God could be as real as I wanted Him to be in my life, and I also realized that it is not a bad thing to be holy. The song says: *Be ye holy, holy, for the Lord God Almighty is holy.*

Be ye holy, holy, for holy, holy is the Lord.

Aren't we as Christian teenagers supposed to like the Lord? The Bible says that the Lord is holy, so I guess that means that we should be holy, too. In Leviticus 20:7, we find that to be holy means to sanctify yourself, or to set yourself apart from the world. If holiness means that we are not supposed to be like the world, then how come as teenagers we do not want to be labeled as the "holy" girls? Are we setting ourselves apart by making the worldly girls our role models?

I picked up a *Seventeen* magazine with Mandy Moore's picture on the front to use as an illustration in my Sunday school class. I looked through her article on "60 Things I Want to Do Before I Am 30." Number one on her list was "shave my head." Number three or four on her list was "cuss someone out." Several times on her list she mentioned certain things she wanted to do because "it would give me so much power and control." Way down on her list was "be a wife and a mother." At least being a wife and a mother made her list, but her goals and desires are way out of line. Yet, this is the girl, along with others like Jennifer Lopez (J. Lo), whom I most hear teenage girls admiring and see them copying.

Are these girls considered "holy" girls? I don't think so; in fact, they are far from holy. They have not set themselves apart from anything except godliness and holiness.

Some teenage girls went up to a girl in my Sunday school class and asked, "Why haven't you been immoral with a guy yet?"

To those girls who asked that question, I say, "You are the reason our country will be destroyed. When the Christian teenagers put no difference between holy and unholy, that makes God very angry. I can only hope and pray that you get your heart right with God before it is too late."

To the girl to whom this question was asked, I say, "You have been set apart for a special purpose and do not EVER be ashamed that you are called 'holy' by your peers, for God also calls you holy."

The truth is, teenage girls, we need a revival among ourselves of holiness, righteousness, and godliness. We need some teenage girls who are not afraid to stand up for right and to be called holy—even if they have to take a stand against their own friends and peers.

Girls, if we get serious about this matter of being holy and set apart, we will also see a difference in the lives of the young men in our schools. You have no idea how much influence you have on the young men in our schools. You have no idea how much influence you have on the young men in your school and in your youth group. If you would decide you want to get serious about serving God and seeing some great things happen in your life, get some girls together to pray, fast, and really get ahold of God. Then you will see not only your life change, but also the lives of the young men in your youth group will change.

Some of you are probably thinking, "This is ridiculous," and you are the ones who need some holiness in your lives the most. Why wait until you are older to serve God and to see Him do great things in your life! Maybe the man you are supposed to marry needs someone to be holy and to pray for him to get his heart right. Are you even

praying for the man you are supposed to marry?

Girls, do not ever be ashamed to be called "holy." In fact, consider it an honor; because after all, God is called "holy" too.

He Loves Me, He Loves Me Not...

"Many waters cannot quench love, neither can the floods drown it...."
(Song of Solomon 8:7)

Chapter Five

He Loves Me,
He Loves Me Not...

Teenagers, for the most part, are very honest, blunt, and frank. They are not afraid to give their opinion and say exactly what they think. So, since I am writing basically to teens, I am going to be very honest, blunt, and frank!

My spending time with teenage girls has made me realize that 99 percent of them (including me just a few years ago) have one thing on their mind: DATING! You may or may not be allowed to date right now, but even those of you whose parents say you are not even allowed to think of marriage until you're 30 (don't worry—my parents said the

same thing!) still think about guys and have one, two, or several in whom you are interested. Please keep in mind that your parents are very wise, and I want you to follow their advice or the counsel of your pastor or your youth pastor; they are always right.

Let me share about two dating couples who were very much alike, yet handled their relationships very differently. Two best friends, Sarah and Holly, were dating Kyle and Tim, who were also best friends. Both couples had been dating for about a year, and both were in love and talking about marriage. Neither their youth pastor nor their parents were very happy with how quickly the couples were going, and both tried to discourage them from dating. However, nothing seemed to be working.

A few months later, Kyle and Sarah broke up after a long argument and many stressful weeks of dating. They decided it would be best to listen to their parents and break up for a while.

Holly and Tim, on the other hand, were getting even more serious and were secretly planning to run away together. Their parents became desperately worried and forced the couple to break up. Holly and Tim were very angry and even more determined to be together, so they decided to run away as soon as possible. They collected all of the money they could find, took their parents' car, and left for a friend's house in another state.

It was getting late, and Tim was getting tired. He kept drifting off to sleep and waking up at the sound of the wheels hitting the gravel on the shoulder of the highway.

"I hope our parents don't find us," Holly said in a worried voice.

"Oh, they'll never be able to keep us apart; our love is too strong," Tim replied in an overly confident voice.

"Tim, that truck is coming right at us!" Holly screamed, but there was no time. A drunken driver ran into their car, and both Holly and Tim were killed.

Their funerals were held on the same day, and they were buried side by side in the cemetery— together like they were determined to be. Parents

wept uncontrollably, and heartbroken friends and relatives came to mourn the loss of these two teenagers who decided to do it "their way."

Now, let me ask you a question: do you think their determination to be together was worth their deaths and the grief of so many people? They just loved each other so much. They didn't even live long enough to find out that God did have a perfect person for each one to marry and a happy life awaiting each one. They never saw it because they did things their way.

We have so many questions about trying to get guys to like us, "stealing" them from our friends, worrying that they won't cheat on us, and the list goes on and on. What we need to realize though is that life is so much longer than just tomorrow and today. All you can see right now is that the guy you like doesn't like you, or your ex-boyfriend is dating your best friend, and the guy your parents don't want you to date keeps calling you. These "mountains" seem so tall that you cannot see around them, but if you could, then you would see that none of those things are really so important. The guy you like will be gone tomorrow, but your parents will be here forever. The friends you are hurting to get that boy to like you are the ones who might really love you and be there for you when you need them most.

The guy you are dating is probably not the man you are going to marry, and if you do not stay pure, the man you were meant to marry may find someone else who has saved herself for him.

You see, life is so much bigger than what is going on today. It's more important than whether or not you are popular or if your clothes are in style or if you are or are not dating. Just remember, God does have one special man for each of you to marry, and He will show you when it is time.

So, sit back, relax, and just enjoy being a teenager!

Princess Practice

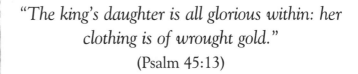

"The king's daughter is all glorious within: her clothing is of wrought gold."
(Psalm 45:13)

Chapter Six

Princess Practice

Dear Girls,

"Once upon a time there lived a handsome prince, and he lived in a castle in a faraway land. Though he had maidens flocking to him, he was very lonely for, you see, he had not yet met his fair princess. He was very lonely, yet he could not seem to find the right maiden for him. His dream of a princess was a beautiful, elegant lady with a gentle spirit and a glowing smile. He dreamed of her day and night, yet she was nowhere to be found."

How many times have we dreamed of our handsome "Prince Charming" coming to sweep us off our feet, and each time we read a story like this we think, "I would be his princess!" We picture ourselves as perfect angels who never speak above a whisper. Yet, the princess story somehow does not seem to apply to our lives right now.

Waking up at 7:45 a.m. when you have to be at school at 8:00 a.m., throwing on some old outfit from the laundry hamper, shoving a donut down your throat, driving like a maniac to school, or yelling at your mom because she won't drive any faster and you are already late isn't exactly what you picture when you think of "Cinderella." Even worse are the times when when you are in a fight with your friend, so you tell everyone what a jerk she is and then flirt with her boyfriend all day long. For some reason, I don't think "Prince Charming" would find you attractive at all.

I know this is the "new millennium" and things are different than they were in the days of castles and kings and queens, but every "Prince Charming" is still looking for his "fair princess." Still, many times it seems like they are very hard to find. A strong, masculine man is looking for a sweet, attractive girl who has kept herself for him.

I hate to burst your bubble, but being the loudest, the boldest, or wearing the most make-up is not going to attract that "Prince Charming" whom you really hope to meet somewhere down the road.

If you want a strong man, you had better be a feminine girl. I don't mean you have to sit and knit all day or know how to cook 500 different meals by the time you are in junior high school! Guys like girls who can throw a basketball through a hoop, too!

Being a princess is really very simple. Just learn to be appropriate in every situation and learn to be a servant. Remember, how you treat your dad and brother now is how you will one day treat your husband.

I think you are all princesses or have what it takes to be one. All you need is a little practice!

Love,

Mrs. Weber

How Do You Want to Feel
on Your Wedding Day?

"…Keep thyself pure."
(I Timothy 5:22)

Chapter Seven

How Do You Want to Feel on Your Wedding Day?

When I was at teen camp one year, Mrs. Jamie Lapina, my youth pastor's wife, talked to the girls about purity. She told a story about an alabaster bottle filled with precious ointment that a mother gave her daughter when she became a teenager. She told her daughter that, like the precious ointment sealed in the bottle, her purity was a very precious gift to be given to only one man—the man whom God had for her to marry. The mother explained that once the bottle was opened and the ointment used, the bottle could never again be resealed, and her purity, once given away, could never be taken back.

Mrs. Lapina continued and told us how the teenage girl began dating a guy and one day became very close to giving up that precious gift, but she had been saved—just like the ointment—for that one special man she was to marry.

She did indeed save herself for that man, and she did keep the alabaster bottle to give to her future husband. Finally, her wedding day came, and midst all of the honeymoon and vacation things was a gift for her new groom to open—the precious alabaster bottle.

A Christian girl attended a public high school where she had to take a stand many times. Of course, she felt very lonely. Every Monday morning a group of "popular" girls would come to her and say, "Did you score this weekend?" They meant, "Were you immoral with a guy this weekend?"

Every Monday morning the Christian girl would tell them "No." The popular crowd would laugh at her until she became embarrassed.

Finally, one Monday morning she had had enough. Once again the popular girls were coming to ask her their usual question, "Hey, did you score this weekend?"

Again she answered "No," and as they began to laugh, she looked right at them and said, "Anytime I want to, I can become like you. But NEVER again can you become like me," and she turned and walked away.

Girls, let me tell you again what she said. Any time you want to, you can become like the worldly, unsaved girls and let a lot of guys steal your purity, but NEVER again can those girls be pure and get back what you still have. Any time you choose to do so, you can stoop to their level and feel like a broken bottle whose ointment is used, but you will never feel as beautiful, special, or secure as those who have saved themselves for one man.

Girls seem to get so desperate about dating, and if a girl doesn't have a steady boyfriend by the time she is in the eighth grade, she does not think she will ever get married. Let me tell you, teenage

girls, it is a thousand times better to wait and save yourself for the "man of your dreams" (who is the man God will give you, by the way), than it is to settle for an average guy, live an average life, and just feel average all of the time.

You see, even the most perverted, defiled boy who has stolen the purity of one teenage girl after another, deep down in his heart wants to marry a girl who is pure.

Let me use the illustration of a rose. Pass around a beautiful rose and let everyone smell its fragrance and touch the soft, tender petals. Everyone gets to enjoy that rose for a few moments. Then, put that rose with a dozen which have not been touched or handled and choose the one you would like to have. The dozen of untouched roses suddenly seem much more beautiful. In the same way, a teenage girl who is beautiful on the inside and the outside and who has never been touched or handled is so much more attractive than the one who has let every guy she met put his hand on her.

Now, some of you may have been abused and

you had nothing to do with it. Let me tell you, and please believe me when I say, that **it is not your fault**. You cannot blame yourself for something over which you had no control.

I am sure there are those of you who may think it is too late to have a happy life and marry the "man of your dreams." Maybe you have already let a boy put his hands on you and touch you, or maybe you have even lost your purity. You may have lost your purity, but you have not lost God's mercy or His willingness to forgive. Some of you are convinced that since you made a mistake one time, God is angry with you for the rest of your life.

Remember, our God is the God of the second chance. The song says,

> *I know the God of the second chance—no matter how I have failed Him, no matter what circumstance. Oh, it makes my heart sing, and it makes my heart dance, for I know the God of the second chance.*

Let me challenge you today to decide from this point on to live a pure and clean life. Decide today that God loves you and that He wants you to be happy. Decide also that you are going to save yourself and trust Him to lead you to the "man of your dreams."

Learn to Take a Stand for Right!

At conferences, the young men are often preached to and told to take a stand, but what about the future wives of those young men? Are we going to help our husband take a stand? How can a young lady help a young man if she cannot even say "No" to an insecure, lustful boy who does not want anything but her body?

A teenage girl was sitting inside a giant auditorium listening to an atheist blaspheme and curse the name of Jesus over and over again. "There is no God," he jeered. The girl happened to be a Christian. She listened to the man for several minutes, and something inside her was saying, "This is not right; someone needs to do something to stop him."

Then she heard him challenge her God and say, "There is no God. If there is a God, then 'God, strike me dead.' " The audience gasped as they heard the man mock God.

The teenage girl was stunned and very scared. Then, very slowly, with all of the courage and strength she could gather, she stood up alone and began to sing in a shaking voice.

> *"Stand up, stand up for Jesus,*
> *Ye soldiers of the cross,*
> *Lift high His royal banner,*
> *It must not suffer loss."*

The people around her saw what courage the teenage girl had, and they stood up with her and began to sing.

> *"From vict'ry unto vict'ry,*
> *His army shall He lead,*
> *Til ev'ry foe is vanquished,*
> *And Christ is Lord indeed."*

By this time, hundreds of people were standing, and soon the whole auditorium—like one mighty army—was sounding out the words:

> *"Stand up, stand up for Jesus,*
> *Stand in His strength alone;*
> *The arm of flesh will fail you—*
> *Ye dare not trust your own."*

When they got through every verse and chorus, a hush went through the crowd. Someone yelled out, "Where's the atheist?"

Another person yelled back, "The atheist ran out the door when the girl began to sing."

Who are you, teenage girl who thinks you cannot make it to the wedding altar? Who are you who feels like you made a mistake and can never be happy again? I beg you today to make a decision that from this day on you will stay pure and clean for the man God has for you. Write it down and make a holy vow to God that you promise to keep. My dad says that a teenager is ready to date only after making that commitment to God.

Should you be dating that guy who just can't

keep his hands off you because he supposedly loves you? Are you letting the girls at school who are immoral make you feel like you are "too holy?" Remember, any time you want to, you can become like them, but never again can they become like you.

Isn't It Exciting?

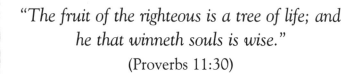

*"The fruit of the righteous is a tree of life; and
he that winneth souls is wise."*
(Proverbs 11:30)

Chapter Eight

Isn't It Exciting?

Recently I went on a trip to the Mall of America. If you have never been there, you definitely should go—it's HUGE! I went with a group of ladies from our church, and one of them was Mrs. JoJo Moffitt. If you know Mrs. Moffitt, then you know she is crazy and loves to have fun, and you also probably know that she is an incredible soul winner. Well, I had never before taken a trip with her, so I did not know just how courageous she was until the van trip to the hotel.

We had been riding on a bus or a train all day, and we were almost to the hotel. Of course, we were all quite tired and were ready to go to bed, then get up, and "Shop 'til we drop"! My friend,

Jennifer Bailey, and I were talking when I over-heard Mrs. Moffitt in the front seat talking to the driver. The man driving our van was about my age (22), and she was talking to him about church. The next thing I knew, she was giving the plan of salvation to him, and I heard her say, "Jesus died for us on the cross—isn't that exciting?" A little later I heard her say, "You can know for sure you are going to Heaven someday—isn't that exciting?"

Then I heard him reply, "That is so exciting!"

At first, he didn't sound very excited, but as she went through the plan of salvation (while he was driving 45 miles per hour down the street), he started to get as excited as she was. Before long, he prayed the sinner's prayer with her and asked Jesus to come into his heart. By the time we arrived at the hotel, both we and the driver were as excited as she was about his salvation!

I really admired what Mrs. Moffitt did and her courage, but of course, I could never do that. After all, she is a lot older and more mature than I am, and she knows all of the right things to say to get people to listen. I think it's great that she is excited about her salvation, but I could never talk to a guy in the van with everyone around and tell him how excited I am that I am going to Heaven, or could I?

Does this sound like the way you are thinking right now? You admire people who talk about Jesus and witness everywhere they go, but you would never do it. After all, it is so embarrassing, especially if the people are rude to you or will not listen. And, after all, what teenager do you know who actually gets excited about "being saved"?

Let me ask you something, teenage girl who wants to stay pure and serve God with your life. If your salvation is not exciting to you, then how are you going to help your husband build that church he is going to build someday with new converts and are so excited about their salvation? If you remember more about the movies you watch than the day you asked Jesus to come into your heart, then please tell me how you expect to make that preacher boy a good wife?

I know some of you are in junior high, and

marriage and serving God seem so far away, but did you know that the way to become a good wife and to serve God is to start now? Did you know that you do not have to be over 35 years old before you win your first soul? Teenagers are, in my opinion, the most fun, the most energetic, and the most exciting people to be around, and that is exactly why they should start winning souls now. They could use all of that energy to get someone excited about going to Heaven someday. And they could use that excitement to get some girls in their youth group pumped up about winning souls. Maybe, if their youth pastor does not have a teenage soul-winning program, he would start one if he thought there were any teens in the church who really wanted to win people.

Maybe this sounds very different to you because you have never won a soul, and the thought of talking to someone you do not know scares you to death! Well, could you get some tracts from your church and maybe leave one on the table the next time you and your friends go out? Could you be really bold and give one to the cashier at the mall when you give him or her your money?

I know this sounds so crazy to some of you, but you really should try it. After my Mall-of-America trip, I decided to try it, and you would be shocked at how many people are so kind and willing to listen. I want to challenge you to give it a try and also to spend some time thinking about the day you got saved. If you think long enough, you might realize how exciting it is that Jesus died for us so we don't have to go to Hell and how exciting it will be to see that person you loved, whom you will never see on earth again but you will see in Heaven one day. Just start thinking, and before you know it, you will be saying, "Isn't it exciting?"

Little Things Are Important

"…Choose you this day whom ye will serve…but as for me and my house, we will serve the LORD."

(Joshua 24:15)

Chapter Nine

Little Things Are Important

As I write this chapter, everyone is back to school and pretty much in a routine again of school, study, sleep, school, study, sleep, school, study, sleep, etc. Cheerleading, soccer season, and semester projects are in full swing, and the dreaded term papers are soon to come!

Some students are new, and some did not come back this year. There are a few new teachers whom you are "breaking in," and the rest are the same ones you have seen from year to year. Your classmates and friends all seem pretty much like you. Sure, you know who the "good crowd" is and

who the "bad crowd" is, but you stay pretty much in the middle—not too good, not too bad. It's easier to get along with everyone that way.

At this point in your life, the choices you are making do not seem "life-changing," and maybe in the back of your mind you know you will one day serve God with your life, but that does just does not seem really important right now. No, your decisions may not seem important, but learning how to make your decisions is one of the most important things you will ever learn.

When I was in junior high school, my friend invited me over to her house to spend the night. Of course, I wanted to go, so I came home and asked my parents if it was okay. All I was looking for was a simple "Yes," but that is not what I got. First of all, the night she asked me to come over happened to be our family night, which greatly complicated matters even more. My dad sat me down after dinner and began a long speech about how it was so important to learn to put my family before my friends and how he did not think it was wise for me to stay all night at someone else's

house. He went on and on, and two hours later
when he was finished talking, he said, "Of course,
it is your decision." Obviously, I had no choice!
My dad, however, was trying to teach me how to
someday make my own decisions.

During my high school years, I dated some
guys, and I would often ask my dad for permission
to go on dates or whether or not I should go, or
even how to handle a certain situation. Every time
I asked him a simple question, I did not get a simple answer, and each talk ended in, "I cannot
make this decision for you; you have to make it
yourself."

I did not have any idea at the time what an
important lesson my dad was teaching me. You see,
now I have graduated and have my own family
and students, and I make little decisions that not
only affect me, but everyone around me, too. If
you cannot make the little, everyday decisions
now, how will you decide where to go to college,
what to do with your life, or whom to marry? If
you can make the so-called little decisions of life
successfully, then they will lead you right into the

big decisions that will affect your future.

If you decide every day to dress right, then you are already deciding to keep your body pure for your husband someday. If you decide to read your Bible every morning, you are deciding that you are going to walk with God and use His wisdom in making your decisions (which is the best way to make your decisions, by the way). When you decide not to go to that party where you know there will be drinking and immorality going on, you are deciding what kind of person you are going to marry and what the standards for your family will be. When you decide to study instead of talking to your friends for two hours on the phone, you are deciding to be a successful person in your career someday.

You see, the so-called little decisions of your life that you are making are going to determine the person you will become. It is incredible, and very sad in a few cases, how very different my life is from some of those with whom I graduated from high school just five years ago. Although most of us are happily married and serving God either here or across the country, in just five short years our "class of '99," who thought we would be together forever, have gone such different ways, and our lives will be forever changed by the "little" decisions we have made.

Teenager, it starts at your age, and the little, everyday decisions you are making are determining what you are going to be five, ten, and even twenty-five years from now. Are your decisions leading you to a happy marriage someday? Are they leading you to a life with no regrets? Are you going to have to tell your child someday that she is deformed because you could not say "No" to that party where you got hooked on drugs?

My first grade teacher, Mrs. Nola Ranft, taught us that the little things are important, and 17 years later, I look back and realize—they are.

Choose Life

*"Who can find a virtuous woman?
for her price is far above rubies."*
(Proverbs 31:10)

Chapter Ten

Choose Life

"And I find more bitter than death the woman, whose heart is snares and nets, and her hands as bands: whoso pleaseth God shall escape from her; but the sinner shall be taken by her." (Ecclesiastes 7:26)

This verse in Ecclesiastes is talking about a woman whose heart is filthy and totally dedicated to stopping others from doing right. She is a woman who is trying to strangle every bit of good that others are doing. Teenage girls, is this verse describing you? Could you apply it to yourself?

"And I find more bitter than death the [teenage girl], *whose heart is snares and nets, and her hands as bands:* [the teenage girl who] *pleaseth God shall escape from her; but the sinner shall be taken*

[destroyed] *by her."*

Are you destroying and stomping out every bit of good that your mom and dad, youth director, pastor, and principal are trying to do? Are you the reason that a young man who had surrendered his life to God has lost his purity and all hopes of some day being greatly used by God? Are you the scorner who makes fun of the teenagers in the youth group who want to serve God?

When I found out that the baby I had been carrying for three months had died, I asked my mom if I should have gone in sooner to see a doctor. She said the only thing the doctor could have done is told me to abort the baby, and I never would have chosen to do that. After I had an operation which removed my baby who had died on his own, the procedure sheet stated that I had a "missed abortion," which means the baby died naturally.

Some of you are aborting or murdering everything righteous and holy around you. Do you believe it is right to kill an unborn child? Then why are you living like that spiritually? You are not only killing everything inside you that is pure, but you are also killing everything and everyone around you who wants to do right.

Ecclesiastes 7:28 says, *"Which yet my soul seeketh, but I find not: one man among a thousand have I found;* **but a woman among all those have I not found**.*"* The greatest tool a man has who wants to do something great with his life is a girl who loves him, stands by his side, and loves the Lord as much as he does.

The greatest enemy and weapon a godly man is up against, however, is a girl who has no interest in anything spiritual and who only really wants to use him. Solomon had 700 wives and 300 girlfriends, yet he said there was not one godly woman among them. Maybe that is why God said, *"Who can find a virtuous woman? For her price is far above rubies."*

One of the saddest, most pitiful things in the world is the thought that there are teen guys who, deep down in their hearts, really want to serve God and give their lives to Him, but they will never do it because of a little girlfriend who only cares about feeling secure and getting as much as she can from "her man."

Girls, right now you have one of the most powerful influences on the teenage guys in your church and school, and what you say and do influences them greatly—whether or not you think it does. I challenge you to get as close as you can—not to your boyfriend but to God—and live the verse, *"Death and life are in the power of the tongue...."* (Proverbs 18:21a)

Are your choices leading you to a life with no regrets? Choose life today and be an encouragement to not only the teenage guys but to everyone around you in what you say and what you do. I choose life…what are you going to choose?